It Could Still Be A Fish

By Allan Fowler

Images supplied by VALAN Photos

Consultants:
Robert L. Hillerich, Ph.D., Bowling Green
State University, Bowling Green, Ohio

Mary Nalbandian, Director of Science,
Chicago Public Schools, Chicago, Illinois

CHILDRENS PRESS®
CHICAGO

Series cover and interior design by Sara Shelton

Library of Congress Cataloging-in-Publication Data

Fowler, Allan.
    It could still be a fish / by Allan Fowler.
        p. cm.—(Rookie read-about-science)
    Summary: Identifies the characteristics of fish and provides
specific examples including the ray, guppy, eel, and seahorse.
    ISBN 0-516-04902-X
    1. Fishes—Juvenile literature. [1. Fishes.] I. Title.
II. Series: Fowler, Allan. Rookie read-about-science.
QL617.2.F68   1990   90-2203
597—dc20   CIP
                                                        AC

How do you know
it's a fish?

If it lives in water,

if it breathes through slits
called gills,

if it uses fins to steer
itself through the water,

and if its body is covered
with scales, it's a fish.

But what if its fins are as big as wings? It could still be a fish

like a ray.

What if it jumps out of the
water? It could still be
a fish

like a salmon.

What if its body is flat
instead of rounded?
It could still be a fish

like a flounder.

It could be as big as a
shark

or as small as a guppy.

It could be a fish, yet look like something else.

An eel is long like a snake.

A catfish has whiskers like
a pussycat.

A sea horse has a head like a horse.

Fish that live in the ocean
are called saltwater fish.

Fish that live in rivers or lakes
are called freshwater fish.

Some people keep fish at
home like shiny goldfish

and tuna

and salmon

and lots of other fish
are good to eat.

So people try to catch them.

What's on the end of this
fisherman's line?

It could be a fish or it
could be an old shoe!

Words You Know

gills

scales

fins

catfish

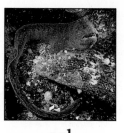

eel

flounder · goldfish · guppy

ray · salmon · sea horse

shark · trout · tuna

Index

About the Author

Allan Fowler is a free-lance writer with a background in advertising. Born in New York, he lives in Chicago now and enjoys traveling.

Photo Credits

© Jeffrey L. Rotman—13, 25

Valan—© Paul L. Janosi, Cover, 4, 7, 14, 20, 23, 30 (top), 31 (bottom left); © John Cancalosi, 5; © Harold V. Green, 6, 22, 31 (top center); © Fred Bavendam, 9, 17, 19, 30 (bottom right), 31 (center left & right); © Johnny Johnson, 11, 31 (center center); © Ed Hawco, 15, 31 (top right); © Robert C. Simpson, 18, 30 (bottom left); © Stephen J. Krasemann, 21; © Thomas Kitchin, 24, 31 (bottom center); © Dennis W. Schmidt, 26; © John Fowler, 27; © Tom W. Parkin, 29

COVER: Blue Tang